THE BARN WEDDING BOOK

How To Hold Your Hootenanny Without A Hitch!

by Neil Smith the Dandy DJ

Copyright © 2018 by Neil Smith Entertainment

Neil Smith Entertainment
2217 Sassafras Drive
Murfreesboro, Tennessee 37128
www.barnweddingbook.com

ISBN: 9781980446286

ABOUT THE AUTHOR

Neil Smith, the DANDY DJ is a full-time professional Wedding and Corporate Event DJ and Photo Booth provider located in Murfreesboro, Tennessee serving the greater Nashville market along with surrounding areas (Kentucky, Alabama, Georgia and more).

Since 2005, he has delighted in helping people celebrate the special moments of their lives and to make the most their gatherings.

Neil is also the author of the books

THE WEDDING DJ BIBLE

How To DJ The Wedding Like A Pro From Preparation To Grand Exit !

PICK A PERFECT WEDDING DJ !

Foreword - BARN WEDDINGS ARE BEAUTIFUL!

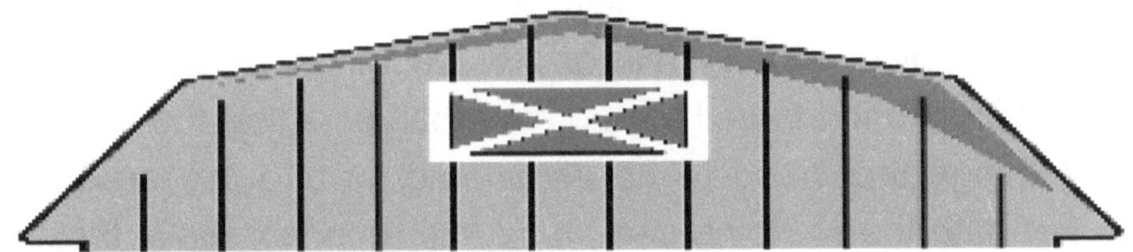

Barn weddings have taken off across America in the past few years and with good reason! They can be much more economical than renting a hotel ballroom (depending upon where you go of course). They bring a sense of comfort and warmth that encourages bonding between families that may be meeting each other for the first time. Pretenses are more easily dropped and you never get a stuffy banquet captain peering over their glasses at you in a judgmental way when you perhaps have a tiny bit more fun than you should! It's like going a few steps up from your backyard without shooting the moon (and your entire financial future) on a bunch of pomp and circumstance that feels more like an obligation than a celebration.

This is why we love barn weddings! You get to let your hair down, make your boots stomp and party with family and friends while making new family and friends. A barn wedding helps your special day feel like a family celebration rather than a committed obligation.

However, with this beauty comes a milk bucket full of things you need to be aware of and prepared for! Things like weather, insects, safety, heat, cold, country roads, electrical power, food service, cake preservation, and how to handle emergencies when you're in the middle of the sticks and nobody has a working phone signal!

These are the reason I have written this book. In Tennessee where I live, about 75% of the weddings I serve are barn weddings and I have learned over the years that there are a lot of things that need to be accounted for and prepared for so that both the wedding ceremony and reception have their best chance at success. This book can help you avoid a lot of the pitfalls I have encountered and teach you How To Hold Your Hootenanny Without A Hitch!

Are you ready? Let's swing the doors open!

CONTENTS

CHAPTER		PAGE
	About The Author	5
	Foreword - Barn Weddings Are Beautiful!	7
1	CHOOSING YOUR VENUE	11
2	VENDORS	27
3	BEATING THE BUGS	53
4	SANITATION FOR ALL	61
5	FOOD	69
6	DIY-ING THE DECOR	81
7	DRESS FOR BARN WEDDING SUCCESS	95
8	WEDDING INSURANCE	107
9	THE BIG DAY	119
10	AFTER THE HOOTENANNY	147

Chapter 1: Choosing Your Venue

- Not All Barns Are Created Equal !

I'm going to start off assuming you already have chosen the time of year you would prefer to have your wedding. This is important to determine before you start venue shopping because the time of year and the weather that accompanies it can have a HUGE impact on choosing the right venue !

For instance, If you have always dreamed of a winter wedding in a snowy setting, you'll need to consider how passable roads might be in icy weather and if the weather is too severe outside, the barn should be more of an actual building that can be shut tight and also has proper heating. I do a few weddings per year where the temperatures take a serious downturn and the planners did not account for providing heat of any sort. Cold guests are miserable guests! Of course there are heaters you can rent should the venue not be equipped, but that really is just one more thing to hassle with on an occasion where you already have plenty on your plate.

Also, if the temperatures take a big enough turn downward, there could be a run on heaters and they may end up being difficult to obtain, even if you've reserved them in advance! Rental places are notorious for overbooking! Hedge your bets and choose a venue that has the heating built in if you're dreaming of a Winter Wonderland Wedding !

Likewise, if you're planning a wedding for the hottest months of Summer or in a region susceptible to rapid temperature changes (like where I live in Middle Tennessee!) you'll want to make sure your venue has AIR CONDITIONING! I do barn weddings in triple digit heat almost every year where I witness elderly guests who have to stay in a running car with the AC cranked until the last moment before the ceremony, just so they can be there in some form, and then immediately leave because the heat could actually be fatal to them! I've also watched people faint in the heat, guests sweat uncontrollably (hot, sticky guests do not want to dance) the tiers of wedding cakes slide and tempers get short. So if there's a chance that severe heat could show up on your wedding day, be sure you've chosen a venue with air conditioning! Also don't forget that if you use any sort of misting devices for cooling, that might be great for guests, but musicians and DJs absolutely cannot have their instruments, electronics and electrical connections exposed to moisture under any circumstance! This is not just for the protection of their expensive equipment, but also for the electrical safety of you and your guests!

Which brings us to the consideration of...

RAIN!

When choosing a barn venue for your rustic dream day, make sure it either has the capability to properly protect you, your guests and your vendors (some requiring electricity) from wet weather! I can't stress enough how important this is! If you're touring a venue and are seeing big gaps of daylight through the slats of wood, this means that when the rain comes down, the insides of that barn will be getting wet. Some barn venues that are more rustic in this way will have large sheets of plastic they roll down from the ceiling on the insides of the walls for protection which usually works just fine. Other venues can be of the position that you just get what you get and that's just "the nature of having your wedding with nature!" Once again, if any of your vendors require electricity and / or have sensitive electronics, this will be an important consideration!

ROADS!

Be sure to note the condition of the roads leading to the venue. Most roads getting to the properties, in my experience are usually fine. It's the roads *"ON"* the actual property which everyone must drive on to get to the areas of the ceremony and reception that can be a challenge! Remember, YOU might have a pickup truck or an SUV with 4-wheel drive but there's likely to be a large number of your guests with basic sedans and economy cars that will find rough roads to be a challenge! There are so many barn venues around my area with unmaintained driving paths on their properties containing huge ruts that must be negotiated just to get to the loading and parking areas, and in rainy weather, these paths can get washed out and turn into mud traps! So when you're comparing venues, be sure to take this into consideration.

CHECK THE ONLINE REVIEWS!

This cannot be stressed enough! Before even scheduling a visit to any venue, check their online reviews. Check them in multiple places. Do an internet search for the venue and read reviews that are not posted on their website. Instead look for Google reviews, Wedding Wire, The Knot and similar and see what past clients are saying. If there are little-to-no reviews online, the venue may be very new or may not do many weddings. If this is the case, odds are that they may not have their methods of operation honed very tightly which can lead to a lot of misunderstandings, under-trained staff (if any), insufficient electricity, inadequate preparation for weather, missing attention to detail and important promised items that simply aren't provided on the big day. I'm speaking very generally from my experience with venues that simply haven't done a lot of weddings and hate to paint those newer venues that are doing it right with a broad brush, but it is what it is and this is just my experience from having served at so many of these venues both new and established over the years.

Am I saying to not consider a newer venue that has yet to well-establish itself and doesn't have much client feedback to explore? Absolutely not! I've done weddings at brand new venues that have absolutely knocked it out of the park! But I would take these aforementioned factors into account and would probably not shell out top dollar to have one of the most special occasions of my life at a venue that hasn't been well-tested or reviewed much.

IS THE VENUE OPERATING LEGALLY?

Proper licensing and permitting are important! Just imagine if the venue you booked and placed a large deposit on was suddenly shut down because they didn't conduct their business correctly and instead simply flew by the seat of their pants? It happens quite often actually. In fact, there was a very popular venue close to me that did not properly register and get the correct permits and was suddenly closed leaving many weddings scrambling for a new place! Once again, this is one of those scenarios that is more likely to happen with a newer venue rather than one that has been around for years and years, but it can happen to older venues too when and if the people in charge should start letting things slide and slip through the cracks.

Licensing and permit requirements can vary from municipality to municipality and I probably wouldn't worry too much about this from an older, more established venue, but if you're looking at a newer venue or one that has very close residential neighbors especially, making a call to City Hall just to check that their I's are dotted and their T's are crossed probably wouldn't be the worst idea in the world.

HOW MUCH SHOULD A BARN VENUE COST?

I won't beat around the bush on this one. The answer to how much a barn wedding venue should run cost-wise is that there absolutely is no answer. This can vary wildly according to where it's located, what a venue has to offer, reputation, time of year, day of the week and of course supply and demand. The best guidance I can give on cost is to contrast and compare with other similar venues but also remember and never forget - YOU GET WHAT YOU PAY FOR! If a venue is offering a price that seems too good to be true, you'd better beware because there's going to be a reason. One way or another, you **WILL** end up paying the price either in money, time, energy or frustration. The balance between these factors is what you will need to ultimately weigh and decide upon.

RESERVATION DEPOSIT AND BALANCE REQUIREMENTS

Once you have found a venue that you like which has a date available that works well and you wish to go ahead and secure, be prepared to place at least a fifty percent deposit. Some venues will require less to hold a date. In rare cases, some venues may require more. In almost all cases, the deposit is completely non-refundable and quite frankly, it needs to be non-refundable. If a venue secures their place just for you and takes themselves off the market for your special date, they lose the ability to sell that date to other interested parties. If you should change your mind and wish to back out, you have really hurt their business without this deposit. You can't expect any venue to hold a date without your placing a good amount of skin in the game, nor would it be appropriate to expect such a thing.

You should also expect to pay your balance at least one month prior to the event date. In many cases, the balance could be due several months before the event date. This is also normal, proper and in most cases non-refundable. Just remember, the closer the event date gets, the harder it will be for the venue to replace you as a client. Any venue operating itself professionally and intelligently will never place themselves into a position where they can be left high and dry. This is actually a good thing for you! If a venue is properly protecting itself, it means that they conduct their business correctly. This is a positive sign that they likely conduct the other aspects of their business correctly and that you will end up with a better experience in the end. Embrace it!

SECURITY AND CLEANING DEPOSITS

Security Deposit - This is a deposit that is held by the venue until after the conclusion of the event when the venue can inspect their property to make sure that nothing was damaged during your celebration. A security deposit can be as little as a few hundred dollars or as much as a a few thousand dollars depending on how fancy a venue you have chosen (yes, I have seen some pretty darned fancy-schmancy barns!) and how expensive the items in and around the venue may be. It's best to do a walk around the property the day of the event before things start and take pictures of anything you notice that appears to already be damaged so that you and your guests don't get blamed for it. You'll probably want to designate someone reliable rather than deal with this yourself on your wedding day if you're one of the people getting hitched.

There are a lot of wonderful and honest people who run barn wedding venues, but unfortunately there are also dishonest ones who will seek out any reason they can conjure to keep your security deposit. The real rub on this one is that once the event has concluded, it's usually dark out. At a barn venue, it's usually pitch black out to the point where you simply cannot reasonably walk the property any further than around the barn itself and take stock of the condition of things and whether or not any of your guests may have damaged anything on the property. In other words, you may be in a position where you have no choice but to simply take the property owner's word on something unless you have protected yourself by doing a daytime walkthrough and taking photographs of anything you notice already damaged. I would highly suggest conducting this walkthrough with a venue staff member by your side.

Cleaning Deposit - A cleaning deposit is exactly what it sounds like. It's a deposit you place which the venue keeps unless and until the venue is returned back to the owners in the state of cleanliness which has been contractually agreed upon. In many cases, a venue will offer the option of a lowered cleaning deposit if the people renting the space agree to do the after-event cleaning themselves. This usually means clearing tables, disposing of all trash, carrying away all decorations and sweeping floors. Failure to do so will normally mean kissing the cleaning deposit goodbye. **Please note:** You can also lose a cleaning deposit over any mess your vendors may leave behind. If you hire good, established and well-reviewed vendors, this usually isn't a problem as most true professionals clean up properly after themselves, but just be aware that you are responsible for the vendors you bring in and whatever they may leave behind.

OK, BUT MY WEDDING IS AT A FRIEND'S FARM!!

Ok, so your wedding is happening at a friend or family member's farm and they're not charging you much if anything. Obviously, things like deposits, payments and super formal agreements won't apply. That stated, still be sure to do a thorough investigation of the rest of the above points and resolve any shortcomings before the big day arrives. You DON'T want to leave anything to chance!

Chapter 2: VENDORS - *Getting The Right Ones!*

Wedding Planner - If you have more money than time to coordinate all the various things that go into a wedding, you may want to consider hiring a wedding planner. This is a person who listens to your vision for your special day and specializes in helping you realize that vision while keeping the turbulence down. Think of them as a human shock absorber who deals with all your other vendors, interprets what you want for your wedding and also plays devil's advocate with you to talk you down from ideas that may not be realistically attainable in their professional experience. If you are really trying to save money and don't have the budget for full-blown wedding planning from start-to-finish, there are actually many different levels of service you can usually purchase from a wedding planner. You can pay them a nominal fee for consulting throughout your planning process which means you can call them up and bounce some ideas off of them when you need to. You can also hire just a "Day-Of" Coordinator which is exactly what it sounds like. They come only on the day of the wedding and keep things on track. They corral your friends and family to where they need to be when they need to be there and also act as the liaison between you and your other vendors so that you and your friends and family can simply concentrate on enjoying each other's company. As with any vendor you are considering, research them thoroughly and make sure you are getting someone experienced and trustworthy!

Officiant - This is the more general term for the person who conducts the actual wedding ceremony. It could be your pastor, a judge or any legally-ordained person. You'll want someone who is warm and personable. The best officiants have a way of putting people at ease and helping them enjoy the moment. Since the entire event will be focused around the joining of two lives and families, and this person's personality and demeanor will play a major part of setting the tone for the remainder of the celebration and also how the couple will look back and remember the occasion, the officiant is someone you really want to meet in person and sit down and talk with for a little while. Grab a coffee and get to know each other a bit. It's important. Make time for this.

Food / Catering - I have seen barn weddings serve prime rib and I have seen them serve baloney sandwiches (for the record, I LOVE baloney sandwiches!). I have seen them with wait staff serving plated meals to the guests at their tables and I have seen (and tried sometimes successfully to control) cattle call buffet lines that wrap around the building. And I have seen almost everything in-between done successfully and also crash and burn into a dismal failure.

Obviously some of the examples above are going to be pricier and more involved than others and I certainly hold my own biases and opinions about all of them, but this isn't about what I think is best for YOUR wedding. This is about YOUR vision for your special day. I'm just here to provide my experiences along with the pros and cons I have walked away with.

The Easiest Is BBQ - The easiest for all involved is Barbecue - hands down! Depending on where you are located, this could place different visions in your head, but here in Middle Tennessee it means pulled meats like pork and chicken with beans, slaw, sauce and pickles. Grab a paper plate and get in line! While the thought of this is likely sending shudders down the spines of a few readers at this moment, this food fits like a glove for barn weddings, is often expected and almost universally loved! Consider having a couple of trays of hot dogs and hamburgers for the kids big and small !

As for Vegans… Why in the heck are you inviting vegans to your wedding!? *Just kidding!* It's usually a good idea to also include a pan of roasted veggies for your guests who aren't big on the cluck, moo or oink. It's also a good idea to include veggie trays with the appetizers that are commonly available during cocktail hour. Vegans need to graze constantly or they'll faint.

The Cheapest - The cheapest option will always be one where the guests serve themselves. It's not so much the food that generates the cost as much as it's the staff that delivers it, prepares it, serves it, cleans up after it and hauls away the waste from it. The more of this you are able to eliminate, the more money you will save!

The rub here is that if you have a friend or family member pick the food up, they'll either have to pick it up so early so as not to miss the ceremony, that the food will be cold by the time it's supposed to be served OR they'll have to miss the ceremony to get it there at the right time.

What most people do to strike a balance and not have any loved ones miss one of the most special moments of their lives is to have the caterers simply drop the food off at the proper time. In this case, it will be up to you to have chafing trays prepared with sterno cans or ice beneath to keep the hot stuff hot and the cold stuff cold.

No! The REAL Cheapest! - The real cheapest is to serve light appetizers only. Think deli trays and similar. If you do this, I would suggest having your entire celebration during the daytime, otherwise guests will leave earlier than you may wish so they can get a real dinner before it gets too late.

Having your wedding midday can save you lot on food and drinks because not only will you have less expensive feasible options for food;

it will naturally shorten the duration of the event as people don't tend to consume as much alcohol during the day. This can be a good thing or a bad thing depending on your preferences. If you want children playing games in the fields and desire a daytime family picnic feel where the guests are staying reasonably reserved, this can be perfect. If you're envisioning people dancing up a storm at your wedding however, an evening reception really is the only way to go which (bringing it all back full-circle) means serving a proper dinner. Alcohol also helps the dance floor, but if you don't want drunk people at your wedding but still desire a pumped dance floor, your choice of a quality DJ or band will be imperative.

Hopefully you're starting to see how all of these factors impact one another. The important thing is to be aware of the implications and strike the right balance for you!

Cake - If you remember nothing else about wedding cakes, remember this - ***HEAT KILLS CAKES!*** I have seen so many cake emergencies at weddings simply because nobody considered what heat would do to a beautiful multi-tiered cake! This really only applies in the Summer at a venue without air conditioning of course, but I have seen cake-makers deliver the cake hours before even the ceremony starts at outdoor or unventilated venues in the peak of Summer with absolutely nothing to keep it cooled. I've seen these cakes sweat and I've seen them slide. Fortunately I've never seen one completely collapse but this is usually because I've brought the situation to attention. Often when there's heat in play, the cake cutting was moved up to be done as soon as the grand entrance is completed so those pictures can be captured and the cake can be portioned immediately so as to avert the crisis.

I've also seen insects getting stuck in the cake because frosting was used instead of fondant for the cake covering. I personally am not a fan of fondant. I don't like the taste and I don't like the texture. It's like laying a sheet of rubberized sugar over the cake in my opinion. Give me real frosting and a real moist cake any day of the week. This stated, there are visuals you can create with fondant that you can't create with anything else, fondant will hold the cake together better in heat than frosting and **BUGS CAN'T STICK TO FONDANT!** So if your occasion will be open-air in any way and you want a proper wedding cake, this is one of the rare times I will encourage the use of (ugh) fondant.

Another alternative to beat the heat and the bugs is to simply have a single-tiered cake for cutting which the bride and groom will eat a piece of (and then pack away to freeze and enjoy on their first anniversary) and have a self-serve cupcake table. I personally love this idea because single-tiered cakes aren't susceptible to sliding and collapsing and it's much easier to place protective screens over a small cake and cupcakes to keep bugs off than it is to try and protect some gargantuan work of delicate art, but I have seen it done elegantly with the use of tulle over the cake (and it actually looked really nice!).

As far as protecting from the heat goes - keeping the cake packed in dry ice for as long as possible until the very last second when it absolutely has to be set up and then getting to the cake cutting as early as possible is the best thing you can do in this situation.

OK, but this section is supposed to be about choosing my VENDORS! This all sounds like D.I.Y.!

Ok, you got me there, but I felt that all the information above was absolutely critical to be armed with before reviewing cake makers because you're going to want to address any of these concerns that apply to your situation to see what sort of help they can give you in these areas. It's easy to walk into a bakery, find someone who does beautiful work and makes delicious cakes, but you also have some logistics to work out. A good cake artist can work with you and help you make intelligent decisions for your unique situation. They may offer delivery, dry ice packing or you may wish to tackle these aspects yourself to save some money. My suggestion is the same with any vendor you are going to consider - read a lot of online reviews to learn the good, bad and ugly before diving in with a cake maker. I feel it's best to let them do what they do best and to let them deliver, protect and set up the cake, but I have also seen MANY instances where the cakes were delivered by the cake artist or their staff HOURS EARLIER than they were supposed to be delivered which caused a lot of the problems mentioned above. But once it's delivered and set up and you walk in on the big day and see it there, what can you really do about it? Not a lot unfortunately. This is why researching your vendors before hiring them is so absolutely critical. If you see a lot of online reviews complaining that the cakes were delivered at times that were outside of the agreed-upon delivery windows, this can be a real problem for you depending on the logistics of the wedding.

Beverage Vendor - Before we start down the road of who will be providing the beverages; caterer, bartender or D.I.Y., you'll need to get a handle on exactly what and how much you'll need. The reason you want to figure this out before hiring a bartender or caterer is self-protection because if they are providing the beverages, they will be adding a markup for themselves (and they should since they are doing the work of providing them) and this provides the vendor an incentive to go excessive. The vendor suggesting more than you will likely need also protects the vendor should your guests really go for the drinks because they will look bad if the drinks run out. Unfortunately it's not a perfect science and you can't expect the vendor to guesstimate down to the exact drink, but if you do a bit of research beforehand you can get a rough idea for yourself of approximately what will be needed so that if a vendor suggests way above and beyond, you will know to get a second and third professional opinion before just blindly signing off.

For this, I suggest going online and doing a web search for **"PARTY BEVERAGE CALCULATOR."** I found a great one on the Better Homes and Gardens website. It came right up at the top of the results and had really wonderful and thorough information about knowing your guests, soda, water, beer, wine, full bar and how to calculate it all per your number of guests and their demographics. There are also many others online to double-check your research against.

- **Bartender** - Keep in mind that anyone with an ABC license can bartend legally (at least that's the requirement in my region). What you are seeking with a bartender is their personality and heart to serve. This person will be interacting with your guests the entire evening. They are helping to set the tone of your celebration! It's up to you. You can seek a service that will simply send in a warm body to pour drinks or you can search for the right person who will be adding charm and an extra level of hospitality and yes, entertainment to your occasion. You find this person by seeking personal referrals, reading online reviews and seeing what people have to say about this bartending service. My thought is that if you're going to pay a bartender, get one that adds flavor and personality to your event, not just a drink-schlepping zombie!

- **Music** - There are so many ways to approach this and it all depends on these things: YOUR vision for YOUR wedding, the musical tastes of you and your guests, whether you expect that your people will wish to dance or simply mingle and enjoy each other's company and also your budget. I personally am a Wedding

DJ as my main living. Before I was a Wedding DJ, I was a Wedding Band Leader and also Solo Musician. I have served many weddings where high energy dancing was the focus and I have served many where it was mainly background music to provide ambience for mingling. I have done weddings where it was mainly mingling but there were a few portions of the event where a special dance or two was desired. I've helped at weddings where the bride and groom had an ipod providing background music and people played games, visited and drank all night. What I'm getting at is that there is no right or wrong way to approach this other than knowing your guests and making the appropriate call based on that and your budget.

What I will say is that if you are going to hire a DJ or Musician(s), don't go cheap. You want to make sure the entertainment you are hiring is professional because they actually have the power to RUIN your wedding in so many ways if they don't know what they are doing or set up heavy equipment in an unsafe manner. A great differentiator between pros and non-pros is the ability to provide proof of insurance. Don't be afraid to ask for this because your venue may actually require it and should your music vendor be responsible for injury or damage on the property, you're going to need it! I'll discuss the importance of insurance later in the book.

Shelter and Electrical Needs - It is very important before hiring to determine what needs your vendors may have as far as electrical and shelter and to weigh those against what your venue can provide. For instance, your ceremony's string quartet may not require any electricity to perform, but if you have a very large number of guests, you may want to have your DJ provide sound services for the ceremony and amplify your officiant and maybe provide a couple of microphones for the quartet while they are at it. Or you may wish to use your DJ to provide the ceremony music. If the venue does not provide electricity in the ceremony area you'll need to find out if your DJ has a battery-powered system available. Some do, some don't. Something like this can determine which DJ service you'll ultimately choose (you don't want to run a generator for power during a ceremony. They make a good deal of noise and you'd have to place it so far away that it would be impractical).

That's just one scenario. Another would be simply finding out how many electrical outlets your entertainer(s) for the reception will be needing and if they need to be on their own dedicated circuit. This does not mean their own outlets, this means their own CIRCUIT. If you put a DJ on the same circuit as espresso machines, margarita makers and bounce houses (yes, I've seen all of these at weddings), odds are that you're going to trip circuit breakers, things are going to go dark at the worst possible time (like during the Bride and Groom's first dance) and it will not be the entertainer's fault! Ask your venue about providing a dedicated circuit for your entertainment especially if you are hiring a DJ or an electric band (as opposed to something like an unplugged bluegrass band - I'm from Tennessee. We have those here.)

Also determine if the music provider has any specific shelter needs if you plan to place them outdoors during either the ceremony or reception. Some do. Some don't. Some will provide their own. If your ceremony will be outside on a very hot day (as many barn wedding ceremonies are) your musicians / DJ / Sound service providers are almost certain to need a pop-up sun shade to work under. This is not something that is negotiable. They personally may be able to take the heat, but their instruments and equipment cannot. If any part of your event will be outdoors, ask your vendors if they will be requiring you to provide them with any type of sheltering from the sun. Many bring their own but if you really want to control the aesthetics of your event and have everything look uniform, this is something you'll want to provide instead. Otherwise you can pretty much count on someone showing up with a purple tent that doesn't flow with your wedding's colors and there won't be anything you can say about it because you aren't providing them any sun protection and they can't operate without it. (Of course if the vendor in question is professional at all and has even a lick of sense, they'll have a white pop-up sun shade. But you just never know). One last thought on shelter for your vendors. If it rains, you absolutely must provide them with proper sheltering inside the barn, under a properly-walled tent (these still get very muddy) or an alternate indoor setup area. You can't expect vendors to be exposing their equipment and especially electrical connections to moisture. This is for the safety of them, you and your guests.

- **Photographers and Videographers** - When choosing photographers and videographers it is very, very VERY important that they have extensive portfolios of wedding-specific work available to view on their websites. Since you are having a barn wedding, you should also be looking for portfolios of rustic settings for these weddings. You want to be very careful while reviewing their work however because the world of photography and videography is notorious for some bad apples grabbing the work of others online and then presenting it as their own. It happens all the time. The best way to protect yourself is to research any vendor you are considering, using the same methods I've been pounding on previously in this book. Search for online reviews not hosted on their own website. There should be a long history of them and the providers should have a stellar reputation for incredible work, professionalism and getting the finished product back to the client in a timely manner. Yes, photographers have become a dime-a-dozen these days because everyone with a point-and-shoot hangs out a shingle and suddenly they're "in business." Just remember, the quality of the work is just part of the equation. You also have the quality of the person. Just think about it - If you had a terrible experience working with your photographer or videographer, this is going to leave a stain on the experience you will have later when you go back and try to enjoy the finished products. When you look back at your wedding photos and videos, part of the joy is remembering not just how much fun you had at your wedding, but how fun running off down the road for those sunset shots were. Or the first look, or how your grandmother was treated. I'll just say it frankly here. If you worked with a jerk who was pushy, curt, pompous, etc., that's going to be PERMANENTLY EMBEDDED in the experience of enjoying your final product. If you retain nothing else - retain this:

- **YOU ALWAYS GET WHAT YOU PAY FOR. HIRE QUALITY PEOPLE AND KNOW THAT QUALITY PEOPLE DON'T COME CHEAP. EVER.**

- *One final thought on photographers and videographers: if at all possible if you have the room at your venue, try to designate a good stationing area for the photography and videography equipment. Most people don't realize this, but photographers and videographers have bags and cases that they must set down somewhere as well as batteries that need to be recharged and remote flashes that stand tall on tripods and need to actually go somewhere. When not given a proper area, what usually happens is that they simply throw the bags and cases down wherever they can find an area and often it will look disheveled and cluttered because they are in a hurry to run around and capture the moments of your wedding. Usually these items end up getting tossed next to the DJ's area. Yes, the DJ who showed up hours early and obsessed over making sure everything looked absolutely perfect for your big day just to have some folks walk over and clutter up everything this person just worked so hard to make nice for you. Usually, seasoned professionals will work it out between themselves, but if you cut any corners on your budget and didn't get someone seasoned and experienced, this can sometimes lead to a behind-the-scenes conflict between your* vendors which you may not realize, but can potentially manifest itself in unseen ways that will affect the quality of some of your services. So if you are able, a designated space for the photography and videography baggage and charging needs is an absolute godsend to all involved every time.

Chapter 3: Beating the Bugs!

- *Be Smitten, Not Bitten!*

When you are having a barn wedding, unless it's a really sealed up barn (some are) and absolutely NONE of the fun will be happening outside of this very sealed up barn (highly unlikely) you will have to put some preparation into how you will be dealing with insects.

You would think that any venue which offers itself for weddings would take measures to address pest issues. Some do. Some don't and don't care. Their position is that this is your problem. You are booking a barn wedding out in nature and bugs are just part of the deal. Besides, once you're there it's not like you're going to cancel the event! Yes, it's going to be on you to be prepared so that your beautiful barn wedding dreams don't turn into bug-maggedon!

Preparing the areas - I have seen people show up with a couple of cases (yes I said CASES) of spray can insect repellent about an hour before the ceremony and simply bomb the bejiggers out of the entire property both inside the barn but especially outside wherever the guests will be congregating - especially the ceremony area! Believe it or not, this actually worked surprisingly well for a while. At least long enough to get through the ceremony and remaining daylight hours which is really all you need for the outdoors. After dark, things will naturally tend to focus on what's inside the actual barn.

I've also seen open flame solutions such as tiki torches and citronella candles used very effectively but I would highly advise against using any open flames for reasons that should be blatantly obvious but I'll mention them anyway because some simply don't consider the safety of themselves and others and the results could be tragic and deadly! Think about it. Tiki torches around the property where you will likely have children playing and even adults in a jovial (perhaps inebriated) state. If someone were to take a notion to playing with the torches or even just knock one over, this could start a grass fire that could quickly become a wild fire and cost lives. I'm sorry but open fire is no joke. The same goes for citronella candles although they are not quite as easily knocked over or attractive to play with as a torch, but still. In and around a barn setting, you can usually count on dry grass especially in the Summer. Also dried out wood. Will you be using any traditional rural wedding fabrics with your decor such as tulle and burlap? These are very flammable! Having any sort of open flame at a barn wedding (besides perhaps a beautiful sparkler sendoff with a dedicated person standing by with a fire extinguisher) is just a bad, bad idea! DON'T DO IT!

If the wedding is on a friend or family member's property - If there is no pest protection in the area you are planning your hootenanny for, ask if they would be open to allowing you to purchase a professional treatment for them a day or two before. Perhaps even consider purchasing them a full year of pest protection as a thank you for allowing you to use their place!

Personal protection - You can get really cute with this! Place baskets of personal-sized assorted repellents all around your ceremony and reception areas and decorate them just like party favors! You can put little signs on the baskets that say things like "Be Smitten Not Bitten" "Bug Off" or come up with your own sayings. It's a good idea to include a few different options of both wipes and sprays as well as different brands and active ingredients.

Covering the food - It's a good idea to have mesh covers over any self-serve food that will be sitting out exposed. They look just like little pop up tents but you can still see through them. If a caterer will be providing your hors devours and main courses buffet-style, be sure to ask them about the measures they take to protect the food from insects.

Protecting the cake - I've seen some really beautiful and creative solutions for protecting the cake in a decorative fashion and most of them involve the use of tulle. I've seen tulle lightly laid over the cake in an elegant manner, but you'll want to be careful doing this because in this technique, the tulle mesh actually touches the cake! I've also seen solutions where a ring of wood or even pvc pipe has been hung above the cake with the tulle mesh attached and then the tulle hangs down and attaches to the table around the cake like a tent. This takes a bit more work, but it's beautiful and effective. Also as previously mentioned in this book, a cake covered in fondant as opposed to icing will be less attractive to insects and less-likely to get them stuck on the surface. But then you have to basically chew through a rubberized sheet of sugar on your wedding cake, which is pretty much what fondant is. Sorry for injecting the personal bias here, but I just really dislike fondant in general. But a lot of people love it and there are a lot of artistic things you can do with it that you can't do with traditional frosting, so there you go!

Chapter 4: SANITATION FOR ALL!

Restrooms - Everyone has to go at some point and restrooms are an important consideration for any event. If the venue is providing the restrooms, be sure to take note of what they have, the capacity of the restrooms and weigh this against your expected number of guests. Will it be adequate or do you foresee long lines of people dancing in place or even worse, finding a shrub out behind the barn!

Portable Potty Houses - If your venue does not provide any restroom facilities or if you feel you will need to supplement due to the size of your guest list, you'll need to rent some portable ones. You can get as fancy or as basic as your tastes and budget will allow in this area.

- **How Many?** - To determine how many portable johns you will need, you can do an internet search for "Portable Restroom Calculator" and you will find a number of very easy to use tools that will allow you to input your estimated number of attendees, event duration, expected women-to-men ratio (for weddings these tend to be about equal) and if alcohol will be served (this will obviously increase the amount of usage and need). The calculators will then tell you the estimated number of standard portable restrooms, handicap-accessible portable restrooms and hand wash stations you will need. I suggest plugging your information into a few of them and weighing the results rather than just *"going"* from one resource.

- **Lighting** - Your portable johns are obviously (hopefully) going to be placed decently away from any key gathering areas and as such, once night falls, you'll have to have a good way for people to not only find them in the dark, but also to be able to see what the heck they are doing once they are inside of them! You'll want to provide some signage to help people know which direction to walk and also provide some lighting along the way. You can pick up solar walkway lights very inexpensively at many discount stores. I have even seen them in dollar stores from time to time. If you see these going for a dollar or two somewhere, grab them! Grab a lot of them! For the inside of the johns, battery-powered stick up lights work great and are really all you need. You'll also want to stick a few of those up at the hand washing station if you're providing one (you really should).

- **Odor** - Yes, these are good places for stick-up deodorizers!

- **Accessibility** - If you are expecting any guests who are wheelchair-bound, having an accessible restroom is going to be very important and thankfully they do make them in the portable variety. You may also want to consider a handicap-accessible version if you are expecting very elderly people who may have trouble stepping up into or maneuvering around in a standard portable john.

- **Cleanliness** - We all know that the portable restrooms (and regular restrooms for that matter) can get pretty messy and unsanitary. Not everyone has the best aim, especially when children and / or alcohol are involved. You're going to need a cleaning kit and somebody designated to check on the restrooms hourly if you want to keep a clean and sanitary experience for your guests throughout your celebration.

Washing Station(s) vs. Squirt Sanitizers - If at all possible, provide at least one hand washing station. When you have such a mixed gathering as a wedding, there will be people who need to clean up their children, dab out a stain and some who just really don't want to use hand sanitizer. Hand sanitizer kills all the bacteria it comes in contact with, both the good and bad. It can also dry out skin. This may seem like a small thing to some, but to others it can be important. When renting a hand washing station, make sure it comes with soap and paper towels and don't forget to place a waste can next to it! Which brings us to...

Garbage - If your barn venue does not provide waste disposal (some do, some don't), you'll need to handle this one yourself and this is a very big aspect of any event and one of those hidden considerations and costs that a lot people simply don't think about. I have read recently that the average wedding has a guest list of about 100 - 120 guests and produces approximately 400 - 600 lbs. of waste! This number comes from an article I read in the HuffPo about throwing an eco-conscious wedding so I suspect this number could be exaggerated a bit to pump up the writer's point, but even if this is so, the takeaway here is that the amount of waste generated by a wedding is going to be considerable and somebody's going to have to plan for and deal with it!

Searching online for calculators to determine how many waste cans to plan for depending upon the size of the guest list proved to be a challenge, in fact I was completely unsuccessful at finding such a thing. Therefore when you tour your venue, it's generally best in my opinion to take note of the size of the area you will be using throughout your celebration and figure out from there how many waste cans you will need for strategic placement using just plain ol' common sense!

Whichever poor soul gets picked for checking the portable johns hourly would probably be a good candidate for also checking the waste cans hourly and changing out the liners as needed. A great method for keeping replacement liners handy is to simply place them into the bottom of the can so when one liner is removed, you can just grab another from the bottom of the inside of the waste can. For the hourly restroom cleaning and garbage duties, I suggest choosing someone you really don't like. Ok, just kidding. Actually, I suggest making this a rotating groomsman duty. Each groomsman must make one restroom and garbage round. ***Tip! A wheelbarrow makes for a great garbage bag hauler!***

Another thing you'll need to consider is where to store all the collected garbage bags. My best suggestion for this is an open-bed trailer that can then be hitched to the back of a pickup truck and hauled to the dump. Or alternatively, you can also rent a dumpster and have the dumpster service haul it off for you.

Chapter 5: FOOD !

Food is easily one of the largest expenses of any event. It's possible to wrestle it down to under ten dollars a plate and I've seen it explode to over a hundred per plate depending on how high on the hog people feel like living. One thing is for sure, it's going to be a focal point of the wedding one way or another!

WHAT TYPE OF FOOD?

Self Serve Options:

Self serve is always the best in my opinion. People can just grab exactly what they want and portion according to what is best for them. Also, when the food is self-serve, IF you position the serving tables correctly, you can allow folks to serve themselves from either side of the table in a double line which makes things so much more faster and efficient! Trust me. You want a double line!

BBQ - In my corner of the world (Tennessee, Alabama, Kentucky and Georgia are where I tend to find myself most often), for barn weddings BBQ IS KING! Around here, it's usually served as a pulled meat (beef, chicken or pork) along with buns, a few varieties of sauces (sweet, vinegar-based, Carolina mustard-based and hickory) and accompanied by it's usual sidekicks (baked beans, slaw, potato salad, southern green beans (that have had all the life completely cooked out of them) and sometimes a traditional salad made with lettuce, tomatoes, etc.).

Most barn weddings (in my region at least) tend to gravitate to BBQ for a very good reason. 1. Almost everyone likes it. 2. It's reasonably economical. 3. It's easy to self-serve. 4. Cleanup is a snap (just toss the disposable serving pans away and go).

Of course you can always go fancier with brisket and ribs and chicken on the bone which is great too if your budget allows. Just remember, if your guests are coming to a barn wedding, they're expecting a casual and fun occasion out in the country with family, friends and kids. You don't need to wine and dine them like the Chez Paris, you just need the food to be good (in my opinion).

Filets - If you want something a little nicer than barbecue on your special day and have the budget to accommodate it, the next step up would be serving filets. Filets are generally cuts of meat usually sitting in a sauce of some sort to help keep flavored and moist. These can be chicken breast, pork chops, pork loin, beef brisket and even lamb, veal, turkey or fish. Chicken, pork and beef are the most common though. All of these work well for the setting of a barn wedding, but of course will add to the expense.

Pasta - Pasta is also a very economical choice that is enjoyed by almost everyone and will fill up your guests quickly and easily (perhaps too quickly and easily). If you decide to serve pasta, it's usually best to have the sauces mixed in already. This helps keep the pasta from drying out. Penne and Rigatoni seem to work the best in my experience and a chicken alfredo or a light tomato sauce also tend to be the best to mix in. It's also good to offer a vegetarian pasta perhaps tossed with olive oil, garlic and some vegetables (primavera) for your guests that may want to keep things a bit lighter or perhaps don't eat meat. Which brings us to...

Vegetarian Options - It's always good to consider your guests that may not eat meat and to give them at least one decent option during the main course. A Sauteed vegetable medley is what I tend to see the most with a variety of summer squashes, mushrooms, green beans (not southern-style cooked in pork) and broccoli. Vegetarians are generally aware they are usually in the minority at these types of gatherings and will often take advantage of veggie and nut trays during the cocktail hour to help compensate a bit if the host has made them available.

Caterer-Served Options - This is where we get into "Sky's The Limit" territory as far as options and budget go. If you're going to have a catering staff physically present during the event, they can be as involved as simply keeping the serving tables stocked and removing the empty trays to having staff stand behind the serving table spooning out the portions, to having a person operate a carving station all the way up to having staff serve your guests at their tables by bringing out 3-course plated meals. Once you get into the realm of a catering staff onsite hand-serving your guests, there really is no way to boil the food options down to where I can sum it up into a portion of a book chapter because once you start going there, the sky really is the limit and the options are completely limitless. Having a staff to stock, manage and operate the serving tables so that your family and friends aren't burdened with these chores while trying to celebrate one of your most special life moments is absolutely an expense worth considering working into your budget if you have it. However, in my opinion, when you get into the area of having waiters in tuxedos hand-serve a multi-course gourmet gastronomical journey to your guests at their tables, it sort of defeats the feel of what a barn wedding is supposed to be. At least in this writer's humble opinion.

Food Calculator - Most of the sources I have researched all tend to agree on 6-8 oz. per guests for the main entree. Lean more towards 8 oz. if you are having more than one main entree selection (i.e. a tray of chicken and a tray of pork). Sides will be about ½ - ¾ oz per guest per side and salads will be about 3 o.z per guest.

Food Safety - *This section generally applies only if you and your people are handling the catering aspect of things yourself instead of having a hired catering staff on-hand.*

The last thing you want is people getting sick either at or from your wedding! If you, your family and friends are handling the procurement, setup and serving of the food yourselves, you'll certainly want to brush up on your food safety protocols!

- **Dairy** - I know everyone loves Aunt Margie's coleslaw, Uncle Brad's alfredo sauce and Mom's macaroni salad! However, dairy-based foods can spoil really fast; faster than a lot of other types of foods. Also, a lot of people these days suffer from lactose intolerance. Unless you really have your heart set on a dish that is dairy-based, I would personally do all I could to avoid dishes containing dairy. Exceptions being good, hearty cheese hors devours during the cocktail hour because certain cheeses can be very durable. But if you absolutely must serve food that is dairy-based, then the following section regarding storing and serving temperatures are imperative!

- **Storing and Serving Temperatures** - At the time of my writing this, the FDA recommendations for food storage, transport and serving temperatures are 140 degrees or higher for hot foods and 40 degrees or lower for cold food. This means the cold and hot foods should be transported in well-insulated containers to maintain these temperatures and cold dishes should be placed on ice for serving and hot foods should be in double-layered chafing trays with ignited sterno cans beneath. When double-layering chafing trays over open-flame sterno cans, it's important to keep a layer of water in the lower chafing dish which the other dish then sits on top of. This not only distributes the heat much more evenly, but also protect the trays and keeps them from damage. I would also suggest that whomever is placed in charge of the serving tables be equipped with a food thermometer to continually check the temperatures.

- **Cross Contamination** - Different people may have different food sensitivities and even allergies and we want to make sure to keep them safe. For this reason, be sure that each dish is equipped with it's own serving utensil. Otherwise, you'll have people dunking those big spoons in different dishes and not only will it certainly cause a mess, it could actually get somebody sick. Also keep in mind that single-use plates are going to be more sanitary when going back for seconds than proper dinnerware. Eating on a real plate is always more classy and enjoyable, but disposable will always be safer and besides, this is a barn wedding!

Hors Devours - I know this is a bit out of chronological order, but since the main course is the main focus for food, I felt that should come first and foremost and be the ultimate focus of this chapter. But we can't really leave the chapter on food without discussing the hor devours during cocktail hour.

At most barn weddings I've experienced, the cocktail hour hors devours are generally an assortment of veggie trays, cheese and fruit with perhaps some nice deli meats included with an assortment of breads and crackers to place them on. The idea is to simply provide something light and enjoyable for the guests to snack on while socializing and awaiting the bride and groom's grand entrance, because the main course is generally not made available until the honored couple are present.

Chapter 6: DIY-ing The Decor!

One of the greatest things about barn weddings is that they just beg for fun rustic-chic DIY projects to style them with. And here's the best part - **THEY DON'T HAVE TO BE PERFECT AND YOU DON'T HAVE TO BE A MASTER CRAFTSPERSON!**

Getting Inspired - In my opinion, the best place to start for inspiration is with the family history of the bride and groom. Try to dig back and incorporate personal touches that will give the grandmothers all the warm fuzzies. This can be old pictures, personal trinkets in an old steam trunk, you get the idea. Let your imagination lead you, but be careful not to bite off too many projects. You want your wedding to be fun, not a mile-long to-do list! Also go online and do a search for barn wedding decorating diy. You'll get tons of amazing and simple ideas from Pinterest, Better Homes and Gardens and a never-ending bevy of resources that you could literally lose yourself in for the rest of your life. Perhaps, pick just a couple of resources that grab you and don't seem overly-complicated. Try to keep the special DIY projects down to just a handful and don't be afraid to delegate, delegate, delegate!

Mason Jar Madness - What would a barn wedding be without Mason Jars!? I've seen these jars (could also be Ball Jars) filled with wedding favors, candies, spray-painted on the insides and embellished with burlap ribbons. I've seen them filled halfway with dried beans and then battery-powered tea lights that look like tiny candles dropped into them for use as votives. I've even seen them hung from ceilings with string lights coiled inside of them for decorative lighting. Of course I've also seen them used as drinkware as well as having desserts served inside of them (can you say banana pudding y'all!?). Of course these last two examples mean someone's going to be doing a lot of dishes and as someone who gets stuck with that chore a lot in my house, I can tell you that there must be a special level of Hell where people are condemned to try and clean the insides of these things. They are an absolute pain in the butt to wash! I'd personally just stick to using them for some fun projects.

Signage - If you have different areas down different paths for various points of interest such as the ceremony and reception areas, restrooms, smoking area, photo booth, game area etc. it's a good idea to have some *directional signs* to help point the way. At a barn wedding, most people paint these on arrow-shaped *barn wood slats* nailed to sticks and then stick them in the ground. I've also seen chalk boards used for this as well which works just fine, but there's something about painted rustic wooden slats that adds that special touch for me at least. These don't just need to be used as directionals, they can also have cute sayings on them (Happily Ever After, etc.), the bride and groom's names, wherever the imagination might take you! *Some folks like to use wooden pallets to make signs.* These work great for the event's itinerary showing the approximate times for ceremony, cocktail hour, grand entrance, first dance, dinner, open dancing, cake cutting, champagne toast, bouquet, garter and finally the grand exit! Another great use of wooden pallets if the slats are close enough together, is to paint a nice monogram for the bride and groom.

Wooden Crates - This might be more of a northern thing because I don't see many wooden crates being incorporated into barn weddings here in the South where I live, but in my online research for this book trying to make sure I wasn't overlooking anything, I did notice their use quite frequently in a few different ways. I've seen them stacked on their sides sort of like display cases with flowers and pictures placed inside. I've also seen them used to elevate the wedding cake. So if you're into the look of old wooden crates, that may be something to consider.

Table Centerpieces - This is one of those things where you really can let your imagination go wild, but my encouragement would be that if you're going to have centerpieces with some height to them, have a very broad base with a good amount of weight at the bottom. My better suggestion would be to not have centerpieces that are tall enough to need to worry about being knocked over in the first place. Be a friend to yourself and make life easy.

I have seen centerpieces with mirrors and glass stones as the bases, little metal bird cages with votives, family pictures, lace and burlap, this list could go on and on. BUT the type of centerpiece I like the best which I really feel captures that barn-wedding vibe would be the finished, flat sections of log, usually called "wood slices." Wood slices are also great as platter-bases for the hors devours table. Old timey barn lanterns with battery powered tea lights and / or mason jar votives really finish off this look in my opinion, but that's really all it is - my opinion. This is *YOUR* special occasion and it calls for your personality. The table centerpieces are really one of those areas where you get to be so creative and really make it personal.

Flowers - Flowers are such an integral part of almost every wedding. From ceremony boutonnieres and bridesmaids bouquets, to blooms and petals on the cake to accent pieces throughout the venue and table centerpieces and finally the Bride's bouquet toss, it's hard to imagine a wedding without flowers. But don't just go with your heart on this one. In order to pull off wedding flowers successfully, you really have to approach them from a standpoint of practicality. I know you have been scanning endless perfect displays on Pinterest for months, but you have to consider what's actually going to look good in YOUR specific venue, what's going to be reliably in season for YOUR region and what will hold up in YOUR climate. Trust me, you don't want arrangements you'll have to have someone spraying all day just to keep from wilting. My suggestion on flowers would be to sit down in-person with a few different florists, have a set budget and talk about your venue and the time of year and take in their advice. As always, research online reviews from multiple sources before ultimately choosing which vendor you will ultimately work with.

Guest Sign In Table - Wow! Have I seen some interesting and unique guest sign-in table creations! I've seen murals, logs and artwork for guests to sign. I've seen cards that are signed with special sentiments and dropped into decorative wire cages. I've even seen guests sign flat little wooden hearts and drop them into a PLINKO GAME! The sky's the limit on this one. Let your imagination run wild and have fun! Or you could also go for more traditional elegance with a sign in book surrounded by pictures of the bride and groom if you want to be all boring like that I suppose...

Straw Bales - I encounter bales of straw covered with rugs and blankets used as ceremony seating a lot. It makes for a fun, relaxed atmosphere and really looks great in pictures. Also stacked up in decorative ways around the outside of the barn always adds a really nice touch. One of the best and most fun uses of straw bales I've seen though has been making a seating area and background for a photo booth area. It's easy to hang almost any kind of signage from a bale of straw. Just stick in a piece of wire. I generally don't suggest bringing the bales directly into the reception area however because they do tend to generate dust and track all over the place which generally isn't a good idea around food and drinks.

Barrels - Barrels are big, clunky, heavy, tough to transport and a pain in the backside to deal with in general. That stated, they look amazing as cake tables, cocktail tables, floral displays and decor in general. It's usually best if the venue already has these rather than you trying to figure out how to deal with them because they are basically pieces of furniture. You may also be able to rent them from a local event supply company where you would / could also rent your tables, chairs, portable toilets, dance floor, etc if needed.

Corrugated Tubs and Buckets - These things look great and work great as drink wells. Fill them with ice and bottles of beverages (water, soda, beer, little fruity wine coolers) and let your guests serve themselves. Keep in mind that there will most certainly be some water runoff from these things just from people pulling drinks out of the ice water and especially if there happen to be any leaks in these tubs. Keep these things away from main walkways and especially away from electrical sources (including wires being run on the ground) and your vendors that may rely on the electricity such as your DJ or band. They cannot safely operate standing in a pool of water and most will (rightfully) refuse to do so. If placing these tubs in the grass is an option, this would be your best one. Otherwise, just place strategically and safely. Corrugated buckets and tubs also work great for floral arrangements.

String Lights - Looking for a simple, soft and inexpensive way to illuminate different areas from overhead or to just add accents behind some sheer draping? String lights to the rescue! They're easy to hang and they add almost a firefly-like ambience to the night! I'm talking about elegant white string light, not multi-colored Christmas lights. Don't go there. We want barn elegance, not lazy hillbilly who forgot to take their holiday decorations off the porch!

Fabrics! Burlap, Lace and Tulle Oh My! - These fabrics are staples in the barn wedding world! I see burlap mainly used as table runners more than anything else, but if you're really handy you can make flowers and all sorts of little crafty embellishments out of it. I've also seen burlap curtains. Those never seem to turn out all that great in my opinion though. Often when used as a table runner, there will also be another more lacey type of fabric that will go on top of it to complete the look. I see lace incorporated mostly to accent the table runners and also in the table centerpieces. Tulle is "THE TOOL" for softening up a barn, quickly, cheaply and elegantly! It is something you can use almost anywhere. It can be used for draping over windows and walls. You can make all sorts of accents with it and can even place string lights behind it for a really nice softened glow wherever you decide to hang it.

Fire Safety - As long as we're on the subject of very wisty, dry and fibrous fabrics, I figured this would be a good place to say a word or two about fire safety. A barn is almost always made of wood and many of the decorations in a barn wedding are ones that could ignite very, very easily. I would highly suggest - no strike that - **BEG THAT YOU DO NOT HAVE ANY TYPE OF OPEN FLAMES PERIOD!** This means no real candles. This means a designated outside smoking area away from the barn that is well-lit and cleared with a proper bin for extinguishing and disposing of cigarettes and cigars. I would also highly suggest that you place onto your checklist a couple of fire extinguishers. Make sure they are handy and able to be grabbed quickly in case of an emergency. Now obviously if you're serving hot food from a buffet area, you will likely have some cans of sterno beneath the dishes, but these are well-secured. Just make sure to keep the kids away, blow them out immediately after use and allow to cool before disposing.

Chapter 7: DRESS FOR BARN WEDDING SUCCESS!

Over-All Attire - Stop! No! I don't mean that you should wear overalls! Although that would make for some great pictures. On second thought, if overalls are your thing, go for it!

Dress Code - Before implementing a dress code, take into account what the venue is like (how rustic, terrain, what sort of facilities for staying clean are offered, etc). Also consider the time of year, the expected climate and whether or not the venue has air conditioning or heating respectively. It's fine to want your guests to look good, but it's also important that they be comfortable. Take these factors into account. Once you have decided on a dress code (dressy casual, jeans and boots with plaid shirts, upscale rustic, etc), be sure to include this on your invites and also to repeat it on your email reminders or if you use any sort of online event planning that allows guests to rsvp such as e-vite or similar. It can also be helpful to give your guests a heads up about what the venue is like and also what the climate is like that time of year for those traveling from another region.

Beyond having a dress code, within the parameters of what you have requested, ultimately your guests will wear what they want and there won't be much you can do about that, but below are some thoughts on different types of attire that tend to work well in a barn wedding setting!

Formal Wear Rental

- **Online vs. a Walk-In Shop** - Online rental of formal wear is almost always going to save a bit of money over physically walking into a brick and mortar location, but the downside is that even though you might provide your measurements, it must be shipped to you before you can try it on to see if it actually fits. That involves waiting and possibly mailing back non-fits and waiting some more for another size and possibly repeating that process until the right fit arrives. A physical shop on the other hand, allows you to try on anything in the store right then and there and instantly see how you look. It also allows you to strike a relationship with the people in the shop and get a feel for whether they have an interest in serving and helping you look your best or are just there getting through a day on the job selling widgets.

I'm big on working with people who have an obvious love for what they do and give their clients the attention they deserve and make themselves available for answering questions and giving helpful input. To me, these things are worth their weight in gold. Ask friends for their recommendations, read online reviews and visit the shops you get a good feeling about. I'm just not sure that everything was meant for online purchasing and some things are worth paying a little extra and personally walking into some shops for.

- **Think Small** - Smaller, more kitschy shops are more likely to have unique looks and designs that the larger chain shops who deal in appealing to masses rather than individual tastes will have. A smaller shop is also more likely to have a lot more hands-on involvement from the person or people who actually own the business. This means that this place of business is a lot more likely to be somebody's passion that they pour their heart and soul into. If you don't think these things translate into the way you are served and ultimately the way you will look and feel when you wear the item, think again!

- **Look for a place that does in-house alterations!** - This is especially important if you are renting for your entire wedding party. Someone is bound to find something they love at that shop that works just perfect for them but is going to need just a bit of tweaking. Sometimes these adjustments can be made with hooks and velcro, but a sewn alteration is always preferable!

- **Secure your rentals early** to make sure you can get what you want and aren't competing with every other formal affair in town during peak season. This also gives you more time for the scheduling of fittings and alterations. Also, don't forget to call the rental shop a week before to remind them that you'll be picking your rentals up in just a few days. People even at the best shops do make mistakes and things can fall through the cracks especially in the crush of peak wedding season. Hedge your bets and take the initiative of making sure that not just your formal wear rental providers are on top of things, but also that ALL of your vendors are on top of things about a couple of weeks before the big day!

To Jeans or Not To Jeans! - This should definitely be clarified in the dress code. I've done many a barn wedding where the ladies went for the jeans under the dress look and the guys did jeans with dress shirts, vests and ties and everyone looked fantastic and the pictures were great. I've also done weddings where jeans were mandatory along with plaid shirts and cowboy hats. Jeans are just practical and durable for this type of setting, but ultimately it's a personal choice. If you can't stand the thought of jeans at your wedding, go ahead and let everyone know that it's to be dresses and slacks but to choose with some practicality in mind.

Dresses - Keep in mind that in a rustic event setting there will be dirt, mud, bugs, grass, wooden floors and probably a decent amount of things a person can get snagged on. For this reason, it's usually a good idea if dresses are at least a little bit off the ground and somewhat durable. Seeing as how I'm a guy, I think I'll refrain from offering further advice on dresses besides this tidbit!

Cotton's Not Rotten! Khaki's Not Tacky! - Some of the best barn weddings I have done have had the entire wedding party and family in matching cotton plaid flannel shirts with jeans and boots to round out the outfits. Hey, it works in this setting, but usually only if you have it as a dress theme. And ok, khaki is tacky. I just really wanted to rhyme those two words somewhere in this book. But hey, it's comfortable, durable and semi-dressy so why the heck not!

Belts and Suspenders - Leather belts with big ol' buckles over a pair of jeans! It's a classic, but if you want your occasion to be a bit dressier, putting the guys in suspenders gives a great vintage look that's really going to stand out in the pictures. I mean, you could let them wear just normal belts too, but where's the fun in that!?

Footwear - When we're talking footwear at a barn wedding, a balance of both comfort and practicality are key! You're going to want to wear something you can feel good in all day and night, but also something that can take a bit of dirt and terrain that you won't be falling flat on your face in! Heels are a bad, bad idea and I don't care how short you are! You're likely going to have to walk through some grass and possibly dirt, maybe even a bit of rocks just to get to the ceremony area. Grass can be especially fraught with peril because if there is a divot in the ground, it's easy to overlook and there's a twisted ankle right there, especially for older folks. Barns with wooden floors are notorious for having spots where the planks have a bit of separation in them meaning that a stiletto heel can catch very easily. For ladies, a wedge or a flat is always a good call. For guys, any leather shoe with a good sole or even sneakers if that doesn't offend you too badly. Of course the best option for footwear at a barn wedding is always going to be **COWBOY BOOTS ALL AROUND FOR EVERYONE!** Just embrace it and prepare yourself for some "Yahoo!" here and there.

Hats for Sun Protection - Hey, it's a barn wedding! Go ahead and break out that big ol' sun hat you've been keeping in the closet. If it's going to be sunny and hot and if you'll be out in it for any length of time, you're going to need all the help you can get! Tweed fedoras and newsboy hats are also a great look for the fellas and after dark when the temperature drops, don't forget that most of your body's heat escapes through the top of the head. A good, practical hat can go a long way towards keeping you warm in the nighttime chill! I personally used to wear fedoras all the time and at some point have always managed to crush each and every one of them which is why I switched to the newsboy. My basic black newsboy hat is actually made of a breathable mesh and is just about the best six dollars I have ever spent at a gas station! *(And now you know way more about my personal headwear than you ever wanted to know.)* Of course the best barn wedding hat of all for both ladies and gents will always and forever be the **COWBOY HAT!** *Saddle up Hoss!*

Layers For After Dark - I used to live in San Francisco and the saying around there was that if you don't like the weather, wait 5 minutes and it will change, and that was true. Everywhere I went, I usually carried an extra sweatshirt and light jacket along with a small bag to keep it all in because the temperature would literally drop almost instantly. You don't want to be caught at a special celebration, suddenly the sun goes down and there's a 20 degree temperature change and you're left guzzling rum to keep warm. Even if the daytime is expected to be warm - **jackets and shawls aren't just the law, they're a good idea!**

Chapter 8: WEDDING INSURANCE -

Yes! You Need It!

I don't care if you're having a wedding in a barn or a backyard! Weddings ain't cheap and if you're going to plan something with this many moving parts (things that could potentially go wrong) you'd better have some insurance protection in place! I would highly suggest purchasing a policy that will cover any aspect of the wedding where you may have a significant investment such as if the venue goes out of business, the wedding dress gets ruined, the cake maker disappears, severe illness, death in the family, an act of God makes it impossible for the wedding to take place at all or any number of other factors. Life happens and it always happens when we least expect it.

Wedding insurance is usually very inexpensive. Of course it varies according to how much is included and how extravagant the occasion is going to be, but for your typical barn wedding (at least at the time of my writing this) it's usually just a couple hundred dollars. That's a very small price to pay to protect yourself from the potential loss of thousands of dollars. It needs to be in your budget, simple as that.

Liability Insurance vs. Cancellation Insurance

Typically there are two different types of insurance that cover different aspects of an event, liability and cancellation insurance. You can get one or the other, but in my opinion, you'd be a fool to not purchase both!

Liability Insurance

- **Provides you with protection in case of injuries or property damage** including liquor liability. I'll just go ahead and say it! Serving hard liquor at your wedding is an accident waiting to happen! A very expensive accident waiting to happen. Unless hard liquor is really your thing and you couldn't imagine having your wedding without it, I strongly suggest having nothing stronger than beer and wine.

- **Venues often require a liability policy be in place.** Sometimes the security and cleaning deposits are all that are required, but many venues actually require a liability policy be in place and also that they are specifically named as "additional insured" on the policy. You can usually also add your rehearsal dinner and ceremony locations, if being held on different properties, as additional insured under the same policy.

Cancellation Insurance

- **Vendor Bankruptcy Coverage -** What if a vendor you have placed a significant deposit on, or have even paid in full goes out of business and declares bankruptcy? What if they simply disappear off the face of the Earth entirely? It happens!

- **Wedding Cancellation or Postponement** - If your wedding must be cancelled or postponed due to severe weather, illness or other act of God, you could lose thousands alone on non-refundable vendor payments and deposits!

Additional Suggested Policy Riders - Other aspects I would highly recommend having covered under your wedding insurance policy would be things such as loss or damage to your wedding photos and videos, stolen gifts, damage to the wedding rings, gown and / or cake.

Does A Barn Wedding Cost More To Insure Than A More Traditional Event Space?

I was curious about this one, so I reached out to the nice folks at *WedSafe Wedding Insurance* *(This is not a plug for them. I just happened to be on their website doing research and decided to reach out and ask them a question)* and they were nice enough to email me a very detailed response and here it is: **"No."** Thanks WedSafe for clearing that up!

Do All of Your Vendors Carry Liability Insurance? They had better, or they are vendors you don't want! Ask for their P.O.I.'s (proof of insurance). If they claim to be insured but can't instantly provide you with proof, they are almost always lying. I know that's a heavy accusation, but I stand behind it!

I have seen photographers and videographers jump in and out of bushes during ceremonies, walk backwards in dark rooms with children crawling on the floors behind them, place flashing lights high in the air atop three-legged stands that could easily be knocked over and on top of a guest or potentially damage property. I have seen them place bags in walkways where they could easily be tripped over. Think your photographers and videographers don't need to be carrying liability insurance? Think again!

Let's talk about DJs and Bands! - These are people who will be pulling up to your venue in large vehicles, transporting heavy equipment into your rented venue, setting heavy speakers often 7 feet high into the air on top of three-legged stands and attaching cabling to them which are often routed across doorways and walkways. Now we're going to introduce children, elderly people and often folks consuming alcohol into the equation and if that's not bad enough, we're going to turn out the house lights, fire up colored moving and flashing lights (dance lights) to disorient all the guests and encourage everyone to flail about with wild abandon (otherwise known as white people dancing). **THEN** after it's all over, these vendors who are now fatigued from an entire day of packing, transporting, loading in, setting up and entertaining now have to dismantle all of this setup (often with fatigued children, elderly people and drunken guests still present and active), pack it up, load it out and drive through the property in the dark hopefully without damaging any property or injuring any people. Yet still, I encounter band after band and DJ after DJ that think only fools bother with insuring themselves. This is important folks. Don't hire uninsured hacks. It could be a very, very big mistake!

Should your DJ or Band Provide Proof of Liability Insurance Before You Hire Them?
I'll state this as plainly as I know how and won't

sugar coat this one little bit because it's THAT IMPORTANT! If you hire a band or DJ knowing what you now know about what all they are going to do and deal with throughout the course of your event and fail to obtain proof of insurance from them - **YOU ARE AN IDIOT!** Stop reading this book right now and go get your head checked!

Venues Often Require Proof of Insurance From Your Vendors! - Around my region, many venues actually do play a bit fast and loose with this one, but many don't. I receive last minute panic calls from people somewhat regularly who make the unfortunate discovery that their band or DJ is unable to provide proof of insurance that they somehow overlooked the venue's requirement on. Now it's a week or two before the event and the venue is asking for the vendor POI's (proof of insurance) and telling the folks renting the venue that without them, their vendors won't even be allowed on the property!

Not only do many venues require proof of insurance but also that the vendors need to add the venue onto their policies as "additional insured." Any event vendor who operates professionally and carries proper insurance is aware of this and can easily accommodate this request of the venue. It's as easy as simply logging on to their insurance account, filling in a couple of fields and clicking a submit button. It normally doesn't even cost anything to do. A new proof of insurance is then either instantly downloadable or emailed to the vendor in a matter of minutes. Easy peasy! Any vendor that tries to make excuses about why they can't provide a POI or add the venue as additional insured OR is trying to charge you an extra fee for this basic and common request is either unseasoned, inexperienced, lying or ripping you off!

There is absolutely no reason why any vendor that spends money to insure their business would hesitate to provide proof of insurance! It's a major selling point for them!

INSURANCE - Yes, need it and so do your vendors!

And while we're on the subject of protecting yourself, I wanted to touch on just a couple more safety items that don't necessarily warrant their own chapter, but hey - I have to put them somewhere so here is as good a place as any!

Designated Drivers - Especially in smaller towns where barn weddings occur, police will often post themselves on surrounding roads after dark to look for people driving erratically which could indicate an intoxicated driver. You are more likely to get pulled over in a small town because it's more of a family environment, when a celebration occurs it stands out more than in a heavily populated area and quite frankly, the police simply have a whole lot less to do in a smaller community and your wedding presents them with an opportunity for them to do their jobs and keep their towns safe from those who may not care about the area as much as they and the local citizens do. Sometimes in a smaller town, or even in a larger town for that matter, when there is a celebration taking place that is likely to involve considerable alcohol consumption, Police will sometimes set up sobriety checkpoints nearby. **Don't take chances. Designate drivers.**

Hospital - You're out in the sticks. Nobody has a phone signal. You can't call 911 ! Know where the nearest hospital is.

Chapter 9: THE BIG DAY!

- Go With The Barn Wedding Flow!

The big day is here! You've planned and paid and put things together for months and now everything you have been working towards is culminating and coming together. There are two things you can do at this point. 1. Freak out in a total panic until your wig explodes. or... 2. Go with the flow, take it easy, have fun and if something goes in a way other than planned, laugh it off. We all know the old saying about the best laid plans of barn mice and men. If something is so wrong that you need refunds or to take some other corrective action, unless it absolutely must be addressed right then and there, it can wait until after the honeymoon. This is **YOUR DAY** to enjoy! Make sure that you do, or this is all for nothing.

Day-Of Coordinator - If you have not hired or felt the need for a wedding coordinator but you would prefer to have someone with lots of wedding experience to keep everyone on track and also to act as the liaison to your vendors so as to take that burden off of you, your family and friends, you may wish to consider hiring a Day-Of Coordinator. Most wedding planning businesses will offer just this service (of course expect them to try to sell you on the full-blown wedding planning package) and it may be something you'll want to consider. Having someone to wrangle the troops for the breakfast, makeup, session-scheduling with the photographer, coordinating the first look, lining everyone up for the aisle walks and coordinating all the special moments throughout the reception right up to the grand exit can be worth this extra expense. This service can often be just a couple of hundred dollars. As with any vendor though, do your due diligence and research thoroughly. But if this is not an expense you wish to incur or yet another vendor you feel like researching, if you've hired a seasoned photographer and a DJ who are wedding pros, they already have the rundown of every key point of this event, have done it a million times with and without coordinators and will be accustomed to stepping in and providing guidance on the big day to keep things moving properly. This is yet another reason why you want to avoid going too cheap on your vendors and always hire PROFESSIONALS!

The Timeline

As a Wedding DJ, I receive the full timelines quite frequently from wedding planners rather than just the part that pertains to me. Often these are very detailed so as to keep everybody and everything on track. Below are the items I regularly see in timelines in the order I usually see them along with my observations, tips and suggestions.

Breakfast - Yes bride. You need to eat this. I've seen a few who have skipped this and fainted during the celebration. You don't want to be that bride.

Hair, Makeup and Getting Dressed - Ok, I'm a bald DJ who is also a guy. I'm not usually here for this part, but I will say you want to have areas for people to comfortably get dressed and ready in. The ladies will usually have their own room and the guys sometimes yes and sometimes no. I will say that one thing that is often overlooked in the restrooms at venues would be hooks in the restrooms to hang suit jackets and hats on while getting primped. But that's more of a personal peeve of mine than anything else. Your photographer will likely want to capture images of everybody getting made up.

Vendor Arrivals - The timeline will usually state the expected vendor arrival times. It's usually derived from a combination of your letting your vendors know when they need to arrive by and the vendors letting you know how much time they need for load in and setup.

Pre-Ceremony Photo Sessions - First Look, Family Preparation, individual sessions with various members of the wedding party.

Officiant Arrival - In my experience, the officiant usually arrives about a half hour before the aisle walks begin. Usually one of the first things you'll need for the officiant to do if you are going to have them amplified (which I highly suggest you do) is to have them meet with the person running the sound for your ceremony so that they can get wired up with the lavalier microphone and transmitter pack (the best way to amplify the officiant and vows) and to do a quick sound check. You want to make sure everything is working fine before the big moment. Also during the pre-ceremony time, the Officiant will usually meet with the bride and groom individually to touch base one final time on portions of the ceremony and also to help calm some nerves which is what the best ones are great at.

Ceremony -
- **Call To Seating** - This is usually done by whomever you have helping to keep things on track for the occasion. Quite often the Coordinator or the DJ (if you have hired one) who will also usually be serving as Master of Ceremonies (if you've hired a good one) will call the guests to the ceremony area about 15 minutes prior to the start of the ceremony if they are logistically able to do so depending on how far the ceremony area is from where the guests arrive to the venue at. Otherwise, good signage and the loudest Aunt in attendance usually gets the job done just fine.

- **Aisle Walks** - If you have someone acting as Coordinator, one of their roles is usually getting everybody lined up properly, telling them when to start walking and also giving cues to the DJ or musicians on when to begin the music for each aisle walk. Different DJs and Musicians will handle this aspect of things differently but I can tell you how I, as a DJ handle knowing when to change music for the different aisle walks. Before the ceremony begins, I go and have a key, knowledgeable person from the wedding party physically point out to me the very last person walking in each aisle walk. I then write down their description so that when I see that person walking down the aisle, I know to change the music once their walk has completed. The aisle walks usually consist of **1. HONORED SEATINGS** (parents and grandparents), **2. GROOM, GROOMSMEN AND OFFICIANT** (normally all come out together but sometimes the groomsmen will escort the bridesmaids), **3. BRIDESMAIDS, FLOWER GIRL AND RING BEARER** and finally **4. BRIDE**

- **Ceremony** - You've rehearsed it and done all you can do to make this go as smoothly as possible. Now just enjoy the ride. That's really all you can do at this point!

- **Special Parts Within the Ceremony** - Most wedding ceremonies will include some special part within such as the pouring and mixing of sand, assembling a unity cross, braiding a cord. I have also seen celtic hand-fasting (the bride and groom's hands are tied together with a leather strap) and even foot washing. I have seen bridesmaids sing songs, read poetry and recite scripture. There's really no right or wrong way to do it. Just make it your own and make it special!

- **Recessional** - This is where the Officiant turns the bride and groom around to face the crowd, introduces them as the newlywed Mr. and Mrs. such and such and the bride and groom walk back up the aisle to their special recessional song with the wedding party following. After which usually the officiant will direct the remaining guests on where to proceed from there. If not the officiant, the DJ / Master of Ceremonies will usually step in and give these instructions.

Signing of the Marriage License - The officiant meets with the bride and groom and has them sign the marriage license (sometimes called the certificate) usually immediately after the conclusion of the ceremony.

Post-Ceremony Photography Sessions - These are usually conducted immediately following the signing of the marriage license. The entire wedding party (meaning those who participated in an aisle walk) and other closest family will usually gather around the ceremony area for photo sessions after which normally the bride and groom will go off with the photographers to capture some intimate sunset shots.

Cocktail Hour - While the wedding party and closest family are off with the photographer, this portion of the event, whether involving alcohol or not, is generally known as the cocktail hour. Sometimes this is held in the reception area and sometimes this will be held in a designated section just outside the reception area. There are generally drinks and hor devours available and the time is meant for mingling and for the newly-joined families to get to know each other a little better.

Quite often at a barn wedding there will be lawn games set out to play such as bean bag toss (known as "corn hole" in the South!), giant jenga, big checkers, bolo, ring toss and such. I might avoid games like lawn darts (jarts) or horseshoes seeing as how both of those involve things that could impale a person or at least give them a nasty konk on the noggin!

Whomever your music provider is should be providing some sort of background music during this time for ambience. Make sure that you request that they keep things upbeat. You want to set a celebratory mood now and keep the energy up, otherwise you and your DJ or band are going to have a much harder time filling that dance floor later if you pummel your guests with endless sappy romantic ballad after ballad (which many brides do request not realizing what the ultimate outcome will be).

Reception Seating - After about an hour of mingling, guests are usually called to be seated in the reception area for the grand entrances, first dances and of course, dinner! Sometimes I have served weddings where the bride and groom wish for everyone to start eating immediately as they don't wish to keep them waiting, but usually the food is held off until at least after the grand entrances have finished.

Grand Entrances - This is where whomever is acting as your Emcee for the evening (usually your DJ or Band Leader) will announce the bridal party as well as the bride and groom. Even if you have provided them with the list of names in advance, don't be surprised or offended if the person making the announcements wishes to come line up the wedding party, double check the list and pronunciations and also give instructions on when to enter and where to go once they enter. This is very important because if it goes wrong, the Emcee will be the one that will be left looking like they don't know what they are doing. If you've hired a seasoned professional, trust that they know what they are doing and allow them to do what they do best and make both you and them look good. In my experience, people will often disappear from the grand entrance lineup at the last second or have a name that is difficult to pronounce or will enter before their name is called. All of these things make it look as if the Emcee is doing their job wrong. The only reason I stress this here is because as an Emcee myself, I sometimes encounter confusion on the part of coordinators and clients when I have the list provided to me, but still insist on meeting the wedding party before announcing them. Almost every time I have made the mistake of trusting the list handed to me, it's been wrong and I was left looking like I didn't know what I was doing. Never again.

Bride and Groom's First Dance - My personal feeling is that it is always a better presentation to do this immediately upon the Grand Entrance. All the guests are standing, cheering and focused on the happy couple. The wedding party is on their feet and often standing around the dance floor (because they just entered the room and have not yet gone to their seats) and it just feels like the right time to do this. Otherwise, the music comes down and instead of something happening (which is what one would naturally expect upon such a dramatic entrance), the Bride and Groom just sort of awkwardly wave to everyone for a moment and then sit down to eat while the mood drops from 60 to zero in a flash and either someone comes out to bless the meal or the Emcee instructs everyone for the buffet line or informs them that their meals will be coming out shortly. It's very anti-climactic.

Regardless, quite often the Bride and Groom will make the decision to do their first dance **AFTER** dinner and it's understandable. They've been primped, poked and prodded at all day while being swept from place-to-place. They are ready for a break. They want to get off their feet and have a bite and also don't want to keep their guests waiting any longer.

Both trains of thought on whether to have the first dance before or after dinner have merit and ultimately this is the Bride and Groom's celebration and decision. My opinion is that if at all possible, do the Bride and Groom's first dance immediately upon the grand entrance. It only takes a couple of minutes and provides a much more natural flow to things. You can always do all the other special dances after dinner and that actually would be my suggestion.

Dinner - Almost every barn wedding I have ever participated in has had a buffet line rather than table service. Once the Grand Entrances are complete and the First Dance has finished, if you have a family of faith, this is where your Emcee will announce whomever you have chosen to bless the meal and deliver the microphone to them. Once the blessing is complete, the Emcee will either inform the guests that their meals will be out shortly (if table service) or should provide instruction for the buffet.

Your Emcee should have determined prior to this time whether the Bride and Groom will be served at their table or will lead the buffet line along with their wedding party and closest family so that they can instruct the guests properly. It's often a good idea to have your Emcee walk around and dismiss tables a couple at a time to the buffet rather than telling everyone to get in line at once. Otherwise you are going to have an enormous line wrapping all around the barn. If your Emcee is a member of the wedding band rather than a DJ, they may not be able to walk around and dismiss tables because they will be playing an instrument. In this case, you should have someone designated to release the tables. This is always done best by personally walking to the tables rather than blurting it out over a microphone as if they were at a fast food joint.

Also, if at all possible, have the serving tables situated to accommodate a **_DOUBLE LINE_** meaning that guests can go down either side of the buffet tables. This will get everyone through much faster and reduce the urge for your guests to pretend they didn't hear the instructions, get impatient and charge into the line before being released. I see this happen all the time and it's unfortunate.

Speeches and Toasts - Once everyone has received their meals and has had a few minutes to enjoy them and get settled back into their places at the tables, this is the perfect time for speeches and toasts. You have a relatively quiet and captive audience during this time which you are very unlikely to have for the rest of the evening. Take advantage of it. Typically the speeches and toasts are given by the Best Man and Maid of Honor and will also often include parents and grandparents of the Bride and Groom. If doing a champagne toasts, make sure the champagne has been distributed and people have had the chance to charge their glasses prior to going into this. But honestly, at most barn weddings, people are just raising their koozies and cups.

Remaining Special Dances - Once the speeches and toasts are complete, this provides the perfect time to have your remaining special dances (parent dances). I would highly advise placing them here because if you simply announce that the dance floor is open right after the speeches, it will be very awkward, your DJ or Band will need to get everyone from seated to dancing like taking a car from zero to 60 instantly and it just isn't a good flow.

My better suggestion is to do your **Father / Daughter and Mother / Son dances** here which psychologically places dancing into the minds of the guests and starts getting people into that dancing mood. After this, my best trick to kick starting the dance floor, since most parent dances are ballads is to announce that the bride and groom would like to invite everyone to the floor for a special couples dance. This is a really well-flowing segue between the ballads of the parent dances and getting people onto the dance floor before kicking up the energy. Once again, it's about creating a natural flow rather than brashly shocking the senses.

Open Dancing

It's a good idea to ask beforehand if the DJ or band is open to you submitting a list of some of your favorite songs that you would like to dance to that evening or also just hear during the dinner hour. Believe it or not, there are some arrogant DJs and musicians that are of the mindset that they know absolutely everything and that you should simply leave it all in their hands (hopefully you have eliminated these individuals in your screening process). Likewise, some DJs and bands are fine with you submitting as many advance requests as you like while others will have a certain limit to the advance requests.

There is a good reason why a professional DJ or band may place a "reasonable" limit on advance requests. This is because quite often, one week prior to the event, they will receive a list from the bride and groom with OVER A HUNDRED special requests which is far more than could ever possibly be played in the course of multiple weddings! The time it takes to organize these songs into danceable sets, download or learn the ones they may not already have or know and check them for quality and content (language and appropriateness) when logistically they can't play anywhere near all of them no matter what they do; that's time they may have been able to spend doing other things to make your wedding special! Things such as making a special monogram to appear on their video screens, decorate their setup to match your linen pattern and who knows what other special touches that provider may have been able to prepare! Professional-level DJs and bands are creative people that love to serve and go that extra mile to wow their clients! But if you soak up every extra second of their preparation time unnecessarily, you could actually unknowingly **PREVENT** them from being able to do some of the amazing things that have thrilled their clients so much that they have left them amazing online reviews, which helped you decide on them in the first place!

Please feel free to make all the requests you would like at the wedding and also to email your music provider a week or so in advance with a list of a few keys songs that you would really like to hear along with genres (hip-hop, 80's, oldies, etc). That helps more than you might ever know. But please allow them the breathing room to read the crowd and flow between the right tempos, genres, songs and moods to keep the dance floor going. You've researched and paid for experienced professionals. Let them do what they are best at. Let them do the job you've hired them to do.

Cake - I find it's usually best to do the cake cutting about 20 - 30 minutes or so into the open dancing. People have had a chance to get up, move about, blow off some steam and let their dinner settle, not to mention that the majority of them are still actually present! You don't want to be stuck with a bunch of leftover cake at the end, so this is a great time (the perfect time in my opinion) to do your cake cutting. Be sure to inform your music provider and photographers about 5 - 10 minutes beforehand so they can be prepared and also get your guests prepared to move into that portion of the event.

Bouquet and Garter - Once the cake has been cut, this is usually the perfect time to do the bouquet and garter tosses. This gives the people in charge of the cake an opportunity to portion it up for serving to the guests and also gets all the remaining "special events" completed so that everyone, including the bride and groom can be freed from the structure, pomp and circumstance and just relax for the rest of the celebration. If there are certain guests that have to leave before the conclusion for any reason (age, health, children, etc) they can do so without having missed anything major. And if you're not doing a grand exit and your photographers need to leave by a certain time under their contract *(a money-saving scenario people often utilize),* this completes their portion of things as well.

Bouquet Toss - You'll want to pick a special song for this. It should be something upbeat and fun. Your music provider should be making sure that the throwing bouquet has actually been located before moving into the toss however. I have been asked to announce the Bouquet Toss in the past, done so and then watched the entire room descend into chaos while 20 people scrambled to try and find _"that #%!$ missing bouquet!"_ Therefore, these days before I move into the bouquet toss, I always make sure to ask the Coordinator or whomever is acting as the point of vendor contact on behalf of the Bride and Groom if the throwing bouquet has indeed been located.

Garter - I have found that this is generally done best with two songs; one for the removing of the garter and then one for the gathering of the unmarried guys for the tossing of the garter. One thing I have noticed is that garters shot "rubber band style" don't fly very far although it seems as if they would. Therefore if this can be remembered, it's best for the groom to get very close to the guys before either throwing or shooting the garter because most of the time, it only flies about a foot or two and then fizzles to the floor leaving the guys to have to retrieve it off the ground.

More Open Dancing - At this point in the occasion, things just basically relax and remain relatively unstructured for the remainder of the event. Open dancing, taking requests, mingling, and smoke-em-if-you-got-em (in the designated area only of course!)

Last Dance and Grand Exit

A Last Dance followed by a Grand Exit of the Bride and Groom is a great way to put a nice finishing touch on the reception. I suggest choosing a slow dance as the last dance not only to make it extra special, but also for the purpose of mellowing the energy so that people don't keep wanting to request songs and keep the party going which sort of defeats the purpose of a Last Dance.

Grand Exit - Immediately following the Last Dance, your Emcee should announce instructions for the Grand Exit. Sometimes this is just gathering near the door and cheering as the honored couple make their way to a waiting car. Sometimes it's instructing everyone to grab bubbles or sparklers on their way to gather outside of the building's exit for a bubbly or sparkly sendoff! If doing sparklers, make sure there is a designated (sober) person armed with a fire extinguisher and a water bucket on-hand for extinguishing /

disposing of them. Also make sure the area is clear of anything combustible.

The Grand Exit is also very helpful for putting the punctuation point across to all guests, vendors and the venue that the event has indeed concluded, your vendors can break down at this time and exit the property which can save you from any overtime charges you might incur should you have guests trying to keep the music and party going longer than the time you have purchased.

Vendor Gratuities - It's usually best to create your vendor gratuity envelopes in advance and designate a special person for distributing them before the end of the event so it is not forgotten. I would NOT suggest placing this in the hands of anyone working for the venue, only someone trustable from YOUR party. The people running the venue have a million other things going on and this could be easily and simply forgotten at the end of a long evening.

Teardown / Load Out (How Long?) - Your music provider is at the biggest disadvantage in this area. The caterer and bartender can start breaking down early as the food is put away and last call for alcohol usually occurs about a half hour before the end of the event. But the DJ or Band usually serves right up to the very end of the event and therefore doesn't have the luxury of packing many things early and can't even get to the bulk of their teardown until the event has officially concluded. It's best to make sure to allot a good hour at the end for teardown and loadout for your vendors and also your venue cleanup if it is a space that you are actually in charge of cleaning. It never hurts to ask your vendors how much time they will need for teardown and load out. Most will say about an hour unless it is a very large and elaborate setup with trussing, uplights, projections, etc. If your venue has given you a certain time you need to have the space cleared by, be sure to ask your music provider how much time they require for teardown and load out so you can be prepared.

Chapter 10:

AFTER THE HOOTENANNY

Closing Out With The Venue - Once the occasion is over and the evening has passed, depending upon your contract with the venue, you may need to check in with them about any cleaning or security deposits you may have placed. If you fulfilled the obligations of your contract correctly and your guests didn't destroy anything on the property AND if you did your research properly to begin with and chose an ethical venue to work with that had great feedback from previous clients, you should not experience any issues.

Opening Cards and Gifts - If cards and gifts were received at the wedding or rehearsal dinner, the morning (or day) after the wedding is usually the best time to open them. The newlyweds should absolutely open everything at this time because they may have received something intended to be enjoyed while on the honeymoon and it would be a shame if this were not discovered until after their return! Be sure to make a list of what was received and who it was from because after the Bride and Groom return, they're going to have a lot of thank you cards to write and it would be a terrible faux pas to accidentally thank Aunt Mildred for the macrame socks that were knitted by Grandma Alma!

Past that, the only thing the bride and groom should be thinking about is going off and enjoying some personal time together and having a wonderful honeymoon in whatever form that takes. The rest can wait until the getaway is done and the happy couple have had a few days to return and settle into their new normal life.

Leaving Online Reviews For The Vendors

Your wedding's vendors live and die by their online reviews on websites such as Wedding Wire, The Knot, Gigmasters, GigSalad and Google. If you loved the service you have received, please leave great reviews. That helps others to find great providers more than you might ever realize (it's more than likely that online reviews helped **YOU** find your amazing vendors) and really helps the providers who go above and beyond for their clients to rise to the top and keep doing what they are great at.

Try to refrain from leaving bad reviews unless the vendor really did poorly and you have contacted them about the area in which you felt you were not served well to allow them a chance to try and correct things as much as they can after the fact. There are times when I have been left with egg on my face because a coordinator has asked me to announce certain things like the meal or a certain other portion of the event and I did so not knowing that the caterers weren't yet ready to serve or the bouquet hasn't been found, or the Father of the Bride wasn't in the room when I was told to announce the Father Daughter Dance. Although I have since learned to verify certain things on my own before proceeding with these portions of the event, things do happen behind the scenes and are not always how they appear.

Give the benefit of the doubt if there is any doubt at all because a few things may not go completely spotless on the special day and the vendor you think might be to blame may not be the faulty one at all! One bad review carries the weight of a hundred good reviews.

Of course if the vendor truly and obviously did a terrible job and showed that they just really didn't care at all, then by all means, others need to be warned and that vendor needs to no longer be in business. You absolutely

SHOULD leave a critical review in this case! You might just save somebody's wedding!

Thank You Cards - I know we live in a modern age where online resources exist that will allow you to send out cards with printing that mimics handwriting, but I implore you to make this more personal. These people have taken their time to contribute to and help celebrate the coming together of two families. Although it takes a bit more time, a true personally hand-written thank you card with an actual stamp on it is the only thing that will show the sentiment is truly sincere. Anything short of this is going to ring hollow and only say that this was fulfilled out of obligation and made easier with a database. You don't need to do it all at once. Buy your cards, place them in a stack where they can't be missed alongside the gift, card and attendee list and simply write and send 5 per day until the list is finished, starting with those who contributed time and effort into the occasion, followed by those who gave gifts and lastly those who merely attended.

*****

Thank you for reading *THE BARN WEDDING BOOK! How To Hold Your Hootenanny Without A Hitch!*

If this book has been helpful in any way, please consider sharing with others whom you feel could benefit and of course, leave a great review online!

Now g'wan and git!

Neil Smith of DANDY DJ and PHOTO BOOTH serves a 5 hour radius of the greater Nashville, Tennessee area. Visit the website at http://www.dandydj.com

THE END

www.ingramcontent.com/pod-product-compliance
Lightning Source LLC
Chambersburg PA
CBHW051306250726

48656CB00004B/1513